cabernet
sauvignon

cabernet
sauvignon

a complete guide to the grape
and the wines it produces

dave broom

MITCHELL BEAZLEY

cabernet sauvignon

by dave broom

First published in Great Britain in 2003
by Mitchell Beazley, an imprint of Octopus
Publishing Group Limited, 2–4 Heron Quays,
London E14 4JP.

A CIP catalogue record for this book is
available from the British Library.

ISBN: 1 84000 686 2

The author and publishers will be grateful
for any information which will assist them
in keeping future editions up to date.
Although all reasonable care has been taken
in the preparation of this book, neither
the publishers nor the author can accept
any liability for any consequences arising
from the use thereof, or the information
contained therein.

Commissioning editor Hilary Lumsden
Executive art editor Yasia Williams
Managing editor Emma Rice
Design Nicky Collings
Editor Colette Campbell
Production Alexis Coogan
Index John Noble

Mitchell Beazley would like to thank Oddbins in
Camden Town and Majestic Wine Warehouse in
Docklands for their help with the photography.

Typeset in RotisSansSerif

Printed and bound by
Toppan Printing Company in China

Picture acknowledgements
1, 2-3, 5 Octopus Publishing Group/Alan Williams;
6-7 Octopus Publishing Group/Adrian Lander; 12-13
Janet Price; 15 Octopus Publishing Group/Russell
Sadur; 16-17 Root Stock/Hendrik Holler; 18-19
Janet Price; 20-21 Scope/Jean-luc Barde; 22-23
Scope/Michel Guillard; 25, 26 Octopus Publishing
Group/Alan Williams; 28-29 Janet Price; 30-31
Root Stock/Hendrik Holler; 33 Octopus Publishing
Group/Alan Williams; 35 Octopus Publishing
Group/Russell Sadur; 37 Patrick Eagar; 38-39, 41
Octopus Publishing Group/Alan Williams; 42-43
Janet Price; 45 Octopus Publishing Group/Alan
Willliams; 46-47 Scope/Kactus; 48-49 Octopus
Publishing Group/Alan Williams; 50-51 Janet Price;
53, 54, 55, 56-57, 58-59, 60-61, 62-63 Octopus
Publishing Group/Alan Williams.

contents

introduction

The smell seduces you instantly. There's sweet, slightly
squished blackcurrants, maybe some black-cherry, a
little mint. It smells of fruit, it smells rich and welcoming.
It is, dare one say, what people think a red wine should
taste like. Let's face it, if it weren't for the charms of
Cabernet Sauvignon, most of today's wine drinkers
would be drinking another beverage entirely.

With its deep colour, high tannins, and robust concentration, Cabernet is a variety to be reckoned with. The conditions it's grown in play a part, but it's the physical characteristics of the grape that make Cabernet pack such a powerful punch.

the cabernet look

Skin

Cabernet's skin is blue/black in colour and thick. A red wine gets its colour from its skin, and the thicker it is, the darker the resulting wine will be. The skin will also add tannin to the wine's structure.

Pulp

There's relatively little pulp compared to the amount of skin and the number of pips. This means that the resulting wine will have not only great colour (from the former) but firm tannins (from the latter).

Leaf

If a vine isn't pruned properly it will tend to over-produce leaves, meaning the plant's energy is put into making foliage rather than ripening grapes, and the leaves can shade the bunches from the sun. In cool climates·this can produce a "green" flavour.

Bunch (*see* page 6)

Cabernet produces fairly small, tightly packed bunches of grapes. Too many bunches on a vine will result in a wine that is thin on fruit, and can also give that "green" taste. If the yields are kept low then the wine will have better colour, fruit, and richness.

Cabernet Sauvignon will grow almost anywhere and this, coupled with its sheer flavour-packed nature is one reason why it is now the world's most widely planted quality red grape variety. And it also doubles up as the new wine drinker's favourite red grape. These days Cabernet Sauvignon is made in virtually every country in the wine world.

where cabernet lives & why

However, that's not to say that Cabernet doesn't need certain conditions to reach greatness. It can cope with hard winters, buds late (avoiding late frosts), and needs a good blast of late-summer heat in order to ripen properly. Unripe Cabernet is easily spotted as it smells of grass and green peppers. That said, too much heat has its own problems. Hot-climate Cabernet might give you masses of sweet fruit, but that's all you get.

Great Cabernet Sauvignon comes somewhere in the middle and it's little surprise that most serious Cabernet producers around the world try to find conditions that are as close as possible to those of the variety's home – Bordeaux. That isn't to say that you can only make great Cabernet on gravel, but it does suggest that this is a variety that likes to have warm, dry feet, and soils that aren't too rich.

Preferred soil types

Cabernet may grow anywhere but it performs best on well-drained soils: the gravel beds of the Médoc draw away rainfall as well as retaining heat, which helps with ripening.

The poor soils of Australia, the gravel "benches" of the Napa, and the thin hillside soils of Sonoma, all help to make great Cabernet for this very reason. Put it on cold clay and you'll get a different picture.

Broadly speaking, there are two ways to make wine. You can go all out to capture as much of the character of the grape or you can marry that with the personality of the region, or vineyard. Cabernet can oblige on both fronts, as long as winemakers pay attention to its peculiarities.

cabernet in good hands

It's a small, thick-skinned grape and the more skin there is to juice, the higher the level of colour and tannin. If you are making a fruit-filled Cabernet that is meant to be drunk young you'll want ripe (if not super-ripe) fruit and will leave the fermenting wine in contact with the skins for a short time to get colour but not a huge amount of tannin.

A "serious" Cabernet that is intended to age will be left for a longer time on the skins, allowing the wine to extract more tannins (and in turn get a rich colour). It's a balancing act. You want ripe fruit flavours but not jammy, over-ripe ones; you want structure but don't want the tannins to dry your mouth out when you drink the wine.

This is a grape which loves wood – one of its classic aromas is cigar boxes – and winemakers have long realized that its often sweet-currant flavour melds well with rich flavours from new oak barrels. Most are moving away from the rich vanilla and coconut given by American oak and sticking to French wood.

Cabernet Sauvignon might be most commonly thought of these days as a single varietal wine – there are some tremendous top-end, pure Cabernets from California and Australia – but the fact remains that it is at its absolute best when supported by other grapes.

cabernet blends

Think of it this way. This is a grape with a bold flavour and a solid structure, but that flavour can be slightly monotone, the structure maybe a little *too* firm at times. The other varieties broaden the range of flavours in the wine – and help tone down some of Cabernet's wilder excesses. This is, after all, a grape with a punchy personality.

In addition, Cabernet, even in its spiritual home of the Médoc, can have trouble getting fully ripe in cooler years, or in vintages that are hit by late rains. The Bordelais winemakers – used to often huge variations between vintages – always hedged their bets by planting other varieties, which not only ripened earlier, but which added complexity and roundness to the Cabernet.

Merlot is the main partner, giving softness and plummy notes to the wine. Cabernet Franc (one of Cabernet Sauvignon's parents) adds perfume, while in the best years the late ripening Petit Verdot contributes a wonderful concentrated spiciness and great colour.

While countries that can virtually guarantee ripeness every year tend to go down the one hundred per cent varietal route, the principle of blending has been adopted by most countries and though the Bordeaux blend is the most commonly seen mixture, some other fusions have proved to be highly successful.

In Italy, Cabernet's black fruit and firm tannins work well allied with the cherry-accented Sangiovese. In northern Spain it has been fused with Tempranillo, in Argentina with another Bordeaux *émigré*, Malbec, and in Australia with Shiraz.

Blending works both ways. As well as using other varieties to add to Cabernet's qualities, many winemakers add a little bit of Cabernet to boost their main variety. Those flavours and that structure can do wonders for a nondescript kind of wine – and of course having Cabernet on the label will help no end in selling the final product!

Cabernet Sauvignon was the result of an unlikely coupling between Cabernet Franc (now seen as its lesser brother) and Sauvignon Blanc. Indeed, unripe Cabernet Sauvignon can have some of the characteristics of both its parents.

how cabernet grew up

It appears to have first sprung into being in the Bordeaux region where it was originally known as Petite Vidure. Wines had been made in the region since Roman times, but it wasn't until the late eighteenth century that the great estates of the Médoc began to be created. When this happened the first choice of grape was Cabernet Sauvignon, implying that it had already proved itself as being ideal for the region's gravelly soils and capable of making the high-class wines they desired.

Cabernet remained exclusively a Bordeaux variety until relatively recently. It's no surprise then that when winemakers around the world want to make a serious Cabernet Sauvignon the model they use is the Médoc. It wasn't until the early 1980s that Cabernet really began to spread from its Gascon heartland into the rest of France – particularly to the south. The story is similar elsewhere in the world.

Cabernet had been grown in Spain, Italy, California, Australia, and South Africa since the nineteenth century, but the real change started in the late 1970s when a global wine revolution began to stir. Producers asked themselves why the French should have the fine wine market to themselves and began to make serious red wines, inevitably based on Cabernet Sauvignon. At the same time improvements in technology helped them to make lower-priced, fruit-filled, consumer-friendly wines that they sold not by the name of the region but by the name of the variety. Cabernet with its blackcurrant juiciness once again fitted the bill and the fact that it is relatively easy to grow soon made it the world's most popular red wine.

Tastes in wine have shifted in recent years. Hard tannins are out. Old-style Bordeaux that took a decade to be drinkable is on the wane and in has come a new style of fruit-driven wines.

what will become of cabernet?

The New World is now leading the way, prompting many of Bordeaux's winemakers to change their techniques and produce wines that are more appealing when young.

This shift to fruit is happening at both ends of the price spectrum. Dependable, low-priced, soft, fruity Cabernet will remain – it's grown in virtually every winemaking country in the world and it tastes good no matter where it comes from. That doesn't mean that Cabernet has lost its status as a premium grape variety. For winemakers, it is the variety behind some of the finest red wines on the planet. Planting Cabernet in your vineyard is shorthand for "I am making high-quality modern wines." It's a double-edged sword. Cabernet gives credibility, (and it sells), but its popularity means it can usurp local, and equally interesting, varieties.

There is no doubt that world-class Cabernets are being made outside Bordeaux by winemakers who can cope with its often excessive personality. There are others, however, who still believe that "great" = "huge". It doesn't. Cabernet needs other varieties in the blend. Its appeal is its directness, its flavour, and its structure, but the world's great Cabernets have always had a splash of another grape variety in the mix.

the countries

Cabernet's conquering of the global wine market shows that it will thrive almost anywhere. Most countries have a different take on Cabernet – not only will the climate give a different range of aromas and flavours, but it often needs to be blended with other varieties in order to bring out its best qualities.

When it comes to producing Cabernet Sauvignon, winemakers around the world look to France. And even though the gravelly soils of Bordeaux are the ideal conditions for Cabernet, the French still know the importance of getting the balance right.

france

Top producers

(Some of these producers make blends of Cabernet with other grape varieties; others make one hundred per cent Cabernets.)

All names are Châteaux...

Medoc/Haut-Médoc:
Cambon la Pelouse
Cantemerle
Caronne Ste-Gemme
Cissac
Citran
Coufran
Les Grands Chenes
Lanessan
Potensac
Sociando-Mallet
La Tour-St-Boet

St-Estèphe: Beau-Site
Calon-Ségur
Cos d'Estournel

Bordeaux

It might be one of the world's most famous wine-producing regions, but Bordeaux can't lay claim to be one of the most spectacular looking. The Médoc (the left bank of the River Dordogne that runs from the northern outskirts of Bordeaux to the ocean) is low-lying and featureless – unless you count the hectares of carefully tended vines and the spectacularly grand châteaux. Even though the landscape doesn't impress, there's little doubt that this is a region where money talks.

The wines have been imported into the UK since the twelfth century, when Bordeaux was controlled by the English, though those wines would have been very different to the ones we revere today. The British term for a Bordeaux red, "claret" comes from the French "clairet" meaning a light-bodied and light-coloured red. Though the great Médoc reds have long enjoyed an exalted reputation, it was in the 1960s when winemaking became more consistent. In more recent times, the winemaking regime has continued to change subtly. The hard, tannic wines beloved by the traditional English wine trade are less commonly seen and while great Bordeaux still needs time in the bottle, today's wines have bigger fruit.

The key is striking a balance. Cabernet Sauvignon can give a powerfully tannic wine but tannins don't mean that a wine will get better with age. A wine is a being like your body. The tannins are the skeleton, the fruit is flesh and acidity is the blood. A heavily tannic wine will end up being a bag of old bones; one with tannin, fruit, and acid in balance will mature elegantly. That balance is achieved through blending (of varieties and of different plots of vines), as well as the time the wine is allowed to rest on its skins, and the judicious use of new oak barrels. Finally comes the influence of the vineyard, or commune, where the wine has been made. The soil – and specifically the amount of gravel – and proximity to the sea are powerful contributory factors in creating the range of styles made in this famous region.

It should be remembered that Merlot remains Bordeaux's most widely planted red variety and in areas such as St-Emilion and Pomerol, Cabernet is very much the junior partner. In the Médoc however, it dominates, with each commune offering a slightly different facet of the varity's personality. While bottles simply labelled Médoc should be treated with caution, château-bottled wines from the region can be solidly reliable. The same goes for the wines from the Haut-Médoc that sits on higher ground behind the most famous communes. That said, some its properties make exceptional wines.

Top producers cont.

All names are Châteaux...

Lafon-Rochet
le Bosq
Marbuzet
Montrose

Margaux: d'Angludet
Brane-Cantenac
Cantenac-Brown
Clos de Jaugueyron
Dufort-Vivens
Giscours
d'Issan
Malescot-St-Exupéry
Margaux
Palmer
Rauzan-Ségla
du Tertre

Moulis: Chasse-Spleen
Maucaillou

Graves/Pessac-Léognan:
Branon
Chantegrive
Domaine de Chevalier
Haut-Bailly
Haut-Brion
La Louviere
La Mission Haut-Brion
Olivier
Rahoul

The AC system

The *appellation contrôlée* (AC) system defines the top category of French wines according to their origin. Wines from a particular appellation (defined on the bottle) are made according to regulations that specify vineyard yields, grape varieties, and production methods. Although officially the top-category AC wines are not guaranteed to be the greatest, and some disappointments are inevitable. *Vin de pays* ("country wines") are also regulated, although less strictly than AC wines. They do offer a geographical definition (eg. Vin de Pays d'Oc) and are often labelled by the grape variety. These can be more exciting, modern wines.

The most northerly of the great Médoc communes is St-Estèphe, here the slightly austere, burly wines need plenty of time to mature. There are a number of properties to look out for from this area.

The next, Pauillac, is many people's idea of what a classic, perfumed, cassis, and cedar-accented Bordeaux should taste like and with Châteaux Lafite, Latour, and Mouton-Rothschild as its top wines you can see why. Neighbouring St-Julien makes a beautifully weighty yet voluptuous style when mature; while Chasse-Spleen from Moulis has a richness and freshness that typifies this commune. It's very different to Margaux where the most intense yet perfumed examples come from – high tannins, high acidity, high aromatics, high class, and high price! However, don't forget the south where ripe, elegant wines are made, both in Pessac-Léognan and a more early drinking, fruit-driven style in Graves.

There's more to Bordeaux than that impressive list. In fact the top châteaux are at the pinnacle of a very broad-based pyramid of quality. The region is huge and while the top names are undoubtedly some of the greatest red wines in the world, there's way too much poor-quality, hard, under-ripe, Cabernet Sauvignon-based wine cashing in on the name. The key is not to be fooled into thinking that everything that comes out of this vast area is of the same quality.

Still, if you know your vintages and find a reliable producer/château there are some lovely relatively early drinking wines to be found. Get out there and try them.

The rest of France

The influence of Bordeaux – and therefore the influence of Cabernet – stretches deep into the Dordogne and the Garonne. Regions such as Bergerac, Côtes de Duras, and Buzet are home to an new generation of winemakers (as well as enterprising co-ops), who are paying more attention to quality than their neighbours in the Entre-Deux-Mers, where most of the bog-standard Bordeaux AC comes from. All the regions are slightly warmer than Bordeaux allowing Cabernet Sauvignon to fully ripen in most years and the wines, while still falling within a "Bordeaux" style and made as a "Bordeaux" blend, are fuller and richer.

Bergerac is the region to watch. Home to a generation of new French winemakers as well as UK-born expats, it is making full-flavoured, softly structured reds at great prices. Neighbouring Côtes de Duras is also on the up.

Top producers cont.

All names are Châteaux...

Pauillac: d'Armailhac
Bernadotte
Pontet-Canet
Duhart-Milon
Lafite
Latour
Lynch-Bages
Mouton-Rothschild
Pichon-Longueville-Lalande

St-Julien: Beychevelle
Branaire
Ducru-Beaucaillou
Gruaud-Larose
Lagrange
Léoville-Barton
Léoville-Las Cases
Talbot

Buzet, on the south bank of the Garonne, was another region that Bordeaux turned to in vintages when Cabernet failed to ripen. These days the grapes are going into concentrated, nicely oaked Merlot/Cabernet blends.

Elsewhere in the South West, Cabernet has been used to give fruity sophistication to wines based on powerfully flavoured local varieties. Frontonnais uses it to balance the wild black fruits of Négrette, while winemakers in Gaillac combine it with Duras and Syrah. In the Pyrénéan foothill appellations of Béarn, Irouléguy, and Madiran, Cabernet has been brought in to soften the scarily tannic Tannat.

Cabernet's usefulness as a blender has seen plantings growing throughout the south. It is a major component in the exotic (if over-hyped) Mas de Daumas Gassac from the Languedoc, and is becoming increasingly important in the impressive reds from Provence where it is part of the traditional southern mix of Mourvérdre, Grenache, Carignan, and Syrah.

Meanwhile, in the Midi the unthinkable is happening with single-varietal wines beginning to emerge, made by a combination of local firms (Skalli), Australian incomers (BRL Hardy, Southcorp), and co-ops who have leased out tanks to flying winemakers hired by UK supermarkets. However, a great Cabernet has yet to be made – perhaps due to the vines not coping with overly dry conditions. It could also be due to the fact that, unlike in Bordeaux where the vine has acclimatised to cooler conditions, winemakers in the south need to wait longer for Cabernet grapes to ripen fully and give richer, more alcoholic wines.

Top producers cont.

(All these wines are blends in which Cabernet is commonly, but not always, the junior partner.)

Marmandais: Beaulieu

Bergerac: La Colline
Tour des Gendres

Frontonnais:
Bellevue-la-Foret

Madiran: Barrejat

The South: Mas de
Daumas Gassac
Moulin de Ciffre

Provence: Bas
Calisanne
Mas de la Dame
Revelette
Richeaume
Routas
Domaine de Trévallon
Vignelaure .

Cabernet Sauvignon was the grape that broke the mould of Italian fine wine in the 1970s. It was used first by Antinori, and then by every other serious Tuscan winemaker, to prove a point – that this region could make world-class wines.

italy

Top producers

Piemonte: Rovero

Veneto: Sant' Antonio
Bertani
Serafini & Vidotto
Zenato

Trentino: C.S. di Avio
San Leonardo
Secchi

Tuscany: Antinori
Capezzana
Cafaggio
Folonari
Isole e Olena
Castello di Monsanto
Querceto
Querciabella
Rampolla
Sassicaia
Villa Arceno

Sicily: Planeta
Tasca d'Almerita

What Antinori did with his Tignanello was to blend Sangiovese with Cabernet and age the wine in Bordeaux barrels (*barriques*). Wishy-washy Chianti was replaced by a richly flavoured, well-structured luscious wine, the Cabernet giving much-needed weight and sweetness. Incisa della Rochetta then went one step further and released a powerful, one hundred per cent, *barrique*-aged Cabernet, Sassicaia. The absurdity was that because Cabernet wasn't a permitted variety these "Super Tuscans" could only be called *vino da tavola*. The rules were exposed as absurd and have been changed. These days, Cabernet remains an important element in the Tuscan winemaker's armoury: its black fruits meld brilliantly with Sangiovese's red ones, its tannins are balanced by Sangiovese's acidity.

Great Cabernet also comes from neighbouring Carmignano (in particular from Capezzana), which first planted the variety in the 1960s. It had been growing in Italy for much longer – it arrived in Piemonte in the 1820s, Veneto a decade later. While Frescobaldi in Chianti has had Cabernet growing for over one hundred years.

Piemontese Cabernet can be wonderfully concentrated, but in this cooler northern climate it needs to be planted in the warmest sites. It's found in blends across the north of the country, and it's at its best in Lombardy (where it's blended with Merlot), and Veneto (with Corvina, as well as a straight Bordeaux blend). Some good examples are made in Friuli but they can tend towards the lighter scheme of things. Trentino can make some surprisingly rich, fruity (but not tannic) Cabernets.

In the south Cabernet takes on two roles. As a cheap, fat, sweet varietal drink for supermarkets, or as a serious wine. Look to Sicily for the best of the latter, though the reasons for planting it in the first place are reminiscent of Tuscany in the 1970s. "I planted Cab. in order for people to take my wines seriously," one Sicilian winemaker told me. "Only then could I convince them to try my Nero d'Avola."

The DOC system

In Italy, DOC wines are those of controlled origin, from specific regions, made with specified grape varieties and to regulated styles – it's the equivalent of French AC (see page 24). DOCG indicates even stricter controls, but neither DOC nor DOCG guarantee top quality. IGT is the equivalent of *vin de pays*.

Cabernet Sauvignon might not be the first grape that springs to mind when you think about Spainish wines, but it is, in fact, grown in virtually every region and has been an important element in the renaissance of Spanish wine. If Spanish red is one of your top choices then read on and take note.

spain

Top producers

Priorato: Costers del
Suirana
Mas Martinet
Alavaro Palacios

Penedès/Catalonia:
Augustus
Castell dei Remei
Jean León
Miguel Torres

One of the first wineries to plant Cabernet Sauvignon (in 1864) was Vega Sicilia in what is now Ribera del Duero. The aim? To use Bordeaux varieties alongside the local Tinto Fino to make Spain's equivalent of a great claret. Vega Sicilia is, deservedly, one of the world's legendary wines, the Cabernet Sauvignon helping to give a powerful structure and elegance. Amazingly, it wasn't until the 1980s that other Riberan wineries decided to try their hand.

Though Cabernet can fall prey to the early autumn frosts, it has become an essential element in the region's emergence as one of Spain's cult regions. Another of those is Priorato. Here naturally low-yielding Cabernet marries superbly well with dense, sloe-like Garnacha adding richness, perfume, and tannic structure to wines.

Nearby Penedès, which has always had a cosmopolitan outlook, has long made Cabernet in an international, soft, rich style. The best are from Torres and Augustus. The variety is planted widely in Catalonia but it rarely achieves great heights, the exception being Costers del Segre where Castell dei Remei is the top *bodega* making richly fruited wines. Impressive Cabernet is also made in Navarra.

Elsewhere, Cabernet is very much in its infancy but is already giving a light grape a bit of a boost (Mencía in Valdeorras and Bierzo), filling out the flavour of a variety (Monastrell in Jumilla), or giving another layer of soft richness (with Garnacha in Calatayud and Tempranillo in Toro). Early days but the signs are good.

Top producers cont.

Rioja: Baron de Chirel

Navarra: Chivite
Guelbenzu
Monjardin
Ochoa

Ribera del Duero:
Monasterio
Pago de Carraovejas
Pesquera

The DO system

In Spain, DO wines are those of controlled origin, from specific regions, made with specified grape varieties and to regulated styles – it's the equivalent of French AC (*see* page 24). DOCa indicates even stricter controls, but neither DO nor DOCa guarantee top quality. *Crianza*, *Reserva*, and *Gran Reserva* indicate oak ageing.

Australia's take on Cabernet has always been to emphasize the variety's softer, black-fruited richness. If anything, the dilemma facing many winemakers is making sure their wines aren't too flabby. In recent years there's been a scaling down of overt oakiness and, in the top wines, softer tannins. As winemakers get to grips with the peculiarities of their region, the wider the styles – ranging from "Big Reds" to "Elegant Cabs".

australia

Top producers

South Australia:
Bowen Estate
Chapel Hill
Katnook
Leasingham
Leconfield
McRae Wood
Reynella
John Riddoch
Wynns
Zema
New South Wales:
Bloodwood
Brangaynem
Harris
Huntington Estate
Rosemount

South East Australia

These are the vast, flat, industrial plantings that blanket the irrigated plains beside the Murray and its tributaries. It's hot but the Cabernets from here can lack concentration – the result of high yields and too much water.

South Australia

What has long been considered Australia's premier Cabernet region lies to the far southeast of the state. This is Coonawarra – a long thin strip of glowing red soil sitting on a limestone base. Remember the key to great Cabernet is well-drained soils and a moderate climate. This has it. The wines have gone through a sticky patch: yields were too high and there was a belief that serious wine needed huge levels of tannin. Now they are getting back to their classic best – elegant and rounded, with black fruits galore, a little sprig of mint, and fine tannins. Next door, the new

region of Wrattonbully is being established as a grape farm for the big boys who want its full-flavoured fruit. Padthaway to the northwest makes underrated Cabernet.

The rest of the state's Cabernets, though good, pale by comparison. Best-known for its Riesling, Clare Valley makes some sweet, densely powerful Cabernets often with a hint of eucalyptus. The cool-climate region of Adelaide Hills makes some good examples along its southern border with McLaren Vale and in the cool Lenswood district (where Henschke is situated). McLaren Vale itself produces a resonant, sweet, black-fruited style.

Cabernet is made in the Barossa Valley, but ends up looking like a burly Shiraz. If you like your wine OTT then this is the place for you.

New South Wales & Victoria

On its own, blended with Shiraz or finding its way into multi-regional blends, Mudgee Cabernet is hard to miss. This is one of Oz's most opulently rich, black-fruited (and slightly earthy) Cabernets. Similar levels of immense fruit can be found in the wines from the high-level Hilltops region. Handy if you need to give a blend a bit of oomph, but almost too much on their own. A better option are the intense, minty, blackberry Cabernet/Merlot blends from another high area, Orange – a region to watch.

Victoria has a mass of disparate regions and a wide range of Cabernets. The most elegant come from the Yarra Valley to the northeast of Melbourne. With a long ripening season, conditions are ideal to make gentle (in

Australian terms), refined wines with subtle tannins. In time the Yarra will be seen as one of Australia's best areas for elegant Cabernet. More concentrated, mouthfilling and long-lived examples come from the central regions of Bendigo and the Pyrenees. All age wonderfully, picking up gamey, cedary notes – and need time to age. Though Mornington Peninsula is too cool to ripen Cabernet fully every year, the intense cassis fruit from warm years shows why some wineries persist. The same goes for Tasmania. Cabernet will only ripen if it's planted on the right site – and gets the best weather. When that's the case they are great, stylish, and packed with currants and cedar.

Western Australia

The third (after Coonawarra and the Yarra) of Australia's great Cabernet regions is Margaret River and, for me, it produces the country's greatest examples. Winemakers here don't go for power but for complexity and elegance, with a superb balance struck between the succulent black fruit and integrated tannins. With Merlot, Malbec, and Petit Verdot in many blends, it nods towards Bordeaux but remains resolutely Australian. There are also good examples beginning to emerge from around Mount Barker (Plantagenet) and Pemberton (Picardy), but perhaps it's early days as far as finding out quite which variety(ies) will be the region's best. What is clear is that Cabernet and Merlot make an intense combination here. That's what's great about Australia – there's always somewhere new(ish) and exciting coming along.

The days when drinking New Zealand Cabernet was a masochistic exercise are over. The problem winemakers have faced is the cool climate and those conditions tend to give unripe and slightly leafy Cabernets. So much so that you could be munching on the leaves of a blackcurrant bush.

new zealand

Top producers

Babich
Brookfields
C.J. Pask
Esk Valley
Fenton
Goldwater
Ngatawara
St-Jerome
Stonyridge
Te Mata

It gave the Australians no end of pleasure to brandish one of their super-ripe dense Cabernets in the faces of their Kiwi cousins and say, "This is what Cabernet is about mate. Stick to Sauvignon Blanc." Well, things have changed. Winemakers are stubborn individuals at the best of times and Kiwi ones more stubborn than most.

This young industry has got its head round Cabernet Sauvignon-based reds by quite simply working out where the best sites are to plant the variety. That means stick to the North Island, take it off the too-fertile soils it was originally planted in and put it instead in dirt that will make it struggle. Maybe, if you are lucky (as they are in Gimblett Road in Hawke's Bay), you'll even find some gravel.

Make sure the grapes are exposed to the sun – take off the leaves if necessary – and flesh out the Cabernet with Merlot, Cabernet Franc, and other Bordeaux varieties. The results are hugely impressive. You get the purity of fruit that typifies a New Zealand wine but there's red fruits mixed with the black, finer tannins, and great natural acidity.

Matakana, home of the ground-breaking The Antipodean Cabernet, continues to show promise as does West Auckland. The battle to be top Cabernet area is being fought for by Hawke's Bay, in particular the Gimblett Road area – where superb, plump, supple examples are made and Waiheke Island, where Goldwater makes benchmark Cabernet/Merlot, Fenton adds some Cabernet Franc to the blend, and Stonyridge uses all five Bordeaux varieties. These wines have no vegetal character, no unripe notes, just seamless elegant fruit. The first time I had a Waiheke Island Cabernet I was spitting wine onto Jancis Robinson's lawn with Kiwi author Bob Campbell. The Stonyridge was the only one that stayed firmly inside my mouth.

Despite the recent craze for Merlot, California's favourite
red grape remains Cabernet. Yet it is a relatively recent
phenomenon. Cabernet was first planted in Sonoma in 1878,
but by the 1960s there were only 243 hectares in the whole
state. Winemakers have actually been pretty quick in finding
the right sites and creating a genuinely Californian style.

north america

North California

Why Cabernet? It sells. This is a consumer-driven state.
But also, in California, the grape exhibits a richness not
often encountered elsewhere. These are generous wines
with oodles of black fruit: cherry, blackberry/currant, briar,
plum, even the occasional hint of tobacco.

The Napa Valley is Cabernet's heartland. Napa's greatest
Cabernets don't come from the fertile valley floor but
from the gravel benches on the western side of the valley,
the wind-cooled Stags' Leap on the east, and, best of all,

from the high mountain sites. Both Rutherford and Oakville benches give rich, balanced, black-fruited almost plummy wines. Cool afternoon breezes and poor soil are the main factors behind Stags' Leap's success. Here Cabernet is more charming and opulent with black-cherry fruit and velvety tannins.

The opposite is the case with the mountain sites where small berries and a long growing season give a briary intensity and firmer structure. Continue west over the mountains and you end up in Sonoma Valley. Here gentle but rich Cabernets come from Alexander Valley and the valley floor, but the best, once again, are from up high.

Further north, growers dominate things in Mendocino producing pretty intense Cabernet, with the most richly fruited coming from the untapped potential of Mendocino Ridge.

Top producers

North California:
Rutherford – Frog's Leap
Niebaum-Coppola

Oakville –
Martha's Vineyard
Mondavi
Opus One

Howell Mountain – Dunn

Spring Mountain – Cain
Newton
Togni

South California

Though Napa dominates the Californian Cabernet scene there are some magnificent examples coming from the regions that stretch from the south of San Francisco to the foothills around Los Angeles. One of the greatest comes from a remote vineyard, Monte Bello, high on the Santa Cruz mountain – a concentrated and powerful wine.

Cabernet has now been removed from windy Monterey and has found a better home in San Obispo County where producers in the Santa Lucia Mountains (can you see a theme emerging?) – like Justin and Adelaida – are making blackberry-scented wines. Slightly softer wines are also coming from the eastern side of the county.

Further west, towards the Pacific coast, Carmel Valley produces an elegant, juicily fruited Cabernet, the best of which is Durney. This remains one of California's best bargains, a claim that can't be made for Moraga that comes from the unlikely surroundings of Bel-Air (yes that Bel-Air), and a winery owned by Tom Jones (but not that Tom Jones). It's made in the lush, sweet Napa style and is only affordable to Mr Jones' neighbours.

With all this talk of top-end wines you tend to overlook the fact that seventy per cent of California's wine comes from the huge, irrigated plantings in the Central Valley and that thirty per cent of all the Cabernet in the state comes from the area of Lodi, ninety miles (145 kilometres) east of San Francisco. When yields are kept down, some decent soft red- and black-fruited wines can be made. When greed takes over they end up lean and mean.

There are some world-class Cabernet wines
coming from California, but there is a worrying
trend towards a blockbusting style that obliterates
any difference between site and region. Thick,
sweet, alcoholic Cabernets (the antithesis of Ridge),
reeking of new oak and carrying ludicrous price tags
have become cult wines. It comes down to whether you
prefer American football with its blasts of over-muscled
power or the subtler skills of soccer. Your choice.

The rest of North America

Wine is produced in every state of the USA, even Alaska,
and you can be pretty sure that where there is a vineyard
Cabernet won't be far away. It is making some pretty
impressive wines in Virginia, Arizona, and Idaho, but, out
of the non-west coast states, Texas is one to watch. Bell
Mountain and the high, dusty Trans-Pecos regions both
show good potential. Washington State however remains
the only place to challenge California seriously. Yet here
Cabernet has had a chequered existence. It was the most
obvious red variety to be planted when the major
vineyards were established, but initially it didn't perform
as well as Merlot and it was this variety that became
the fashionable one. The pendulum now appears to be
swinging back. Columbia Valley gives the required long
ripening season for rich, dark wines with a signature
black-cherry aroma, while Red Mountain adds a roast
red pepper note. Ultimately, it will be the blends of the
two varieties that will prove to be the best of all.

Blessed with an ideal climate, Chile is making some of the most outstanding Cabernets around, great-value wines absolutely bursting with fruit. Good news for the consumer, but Chile mustn't rest on its laurels. In Argentina, although Malbec is the more popular variety, there are some superb top-end Cabernets to be found. Chile might rule the mid-market in South America, but Argentina is making waves at the top.

south america

Chile

If you want to discover the most keenly priced, softest, sweetest, most "Cabernet" Cabernet in the world, then go to Chile. The country, blessed with a perfect climate, and disease-free conditions, gets grapes ripe effortlessly, and, allied with intelligent modern winemaking techniques, turns out unashamedly fruit-filled wines. In fact "fruit-filled" doesn't quite do them justice. They ooze fruit, drown your tastebuds in a smile-inducing assault. Chile is doing the same with Cabernet today that the Bulgarians did with the variety in the 1980s, but has taken quality up another notch. This is good news for the consumer who wants a consistent, easy-drinking package. However, it's clear that in the long-term Chile must start to develop a wider range of styles that emphasize the differences between its regions, and make wines with greater finesse. Consistency is one thing, sameness is quite another.

Things are moving on though and it is possible to differentiate between the different regions: the soft, sweet Cabernets from Curicó and Colchagua, slightly tougher qualities from Aconcagua, and the black-fruited power of Maipo. My choice is the wines from the slightly cooler areas of Rapel, where you get intensity and that typical Chilean blackberry fruit but good structure and acidity, and those from Casablanca which, though it is cooler again, may in time prove to be home to the most elegant examples.

Top producers

Chile: Vina Casablanca
Clos Apalta
Montes Alpha
La Palma

Argentina: Archeval Ferrer
Catena
Finca Flichmann
Nieto Senetiner
Norton

There are some top-end wines that fall into two camps: winemakers who have decided that quality means concentrating the fruit more – making huge, dense wines that could collapse after a few years in bottle – and those who are looking not just for fruit, but building an elegant framework around it. The first is commercially sexy, the second is more authentically Chilean.

Argentina

Always a country to do things its own way, Argentina too has picked up the Bordeaux bug, but, rather than joining the rest of the world and planting naught but Cabernet (and Merlot), it has concentrated on the forgotten Bordelais variety, Malbec. As the industry begins to reinvent itself and seek out new export markets so, inevitably, more Cabernet is going into the ground – as we have seen it is the sure way of convincing buyers and public alike of your seriousness – but you also get the feeling that Malbec will remain Argentina's signature wine and that Cabernet will be its support rather than the other way round.

Argentina's main wine-producing region is the high desert province of Mendoza. The dry air, clear skies, warm days and cool nights give ideal conditions to produce intensely fruited wines – as long as the vineyards can be irrigated. The trouble with this is that when over-watered, Cabernet produces a thin, rather wishy-washy kind of wine, a ghost of its normal self. In their rush to make high volumes of "international" wines for the export market, it's precisely what many wineries have been doing. There is a top-end emerging and these wines are well worth looking at. Well-chosen sites, not too high, not over-watered, allow not just Cabernet's signature fruit to shine, but a solid structure to be built into the wines.

While Chile rules the mid-market in Cabernet but struggles to make wines that justify a high price tag, Argentina struggles at the low end but rules at the top.

The rest of South America

Elsewhere in South America, Cabernet is grown in Uruguay and makes good dark-fruited wines. Brazil has plantings but nothing to get excited about. The same goes for Peru and Cuba. Mexico has potential, particularly in Baja California, but has yet to get to grips fully with the variety.

South Africa is currently the most exciting winemaking country in the world. Fact. In the few short years since apartheid was finally banished it has reorganized its wine industry, replanted much of its vineyard, and encouraged a new generation of young winemakers to try and make the great wines the country has always promised. Needless to say Cabernet has a major part to play in this.

south africa

The strange thing about Cabernet in South Africa is that it is both an old-established variety and a new one at the same time. This is, as most of the country's winemakers will tell you, an Old World country in the New World. "Old" South African Cabernet was always made to a French model. The trouble was that the vineyards were badly affected with a vine disease that didn't allow the grapes to get fully ripe. Result? A hard green edge to many of

Cabernets, though great (if often rather severe) wines were made by estates like Meerlust and Vriesenhof during the virus period.

Today the vineyards have been mostly replanted with disease-resistant vines and the difference is astonishing. The dustiness has gone, the green has been banished and in has come mint, cassis, blackberry, and tobacco. It is typified by what happened at Rustenberg where everything – vines, wood, winemaking equipment (and winemaker) – was chucked out. Today it is making one of the greatest new-style Cabernets in the country.

In, too, has come a wider frame of reference. California and Australia are as relevant as Europe and two broad styles are emerging: a rich dense, yet elegant wine (Rustenberg, Boekenhoutskloof, Delaire), and a more structured cassis and tobacco style (Welgemeend, Glen Carlou, Plaisir de Merle). None, however, slavishly follow either a French or Californian model. South Africa is, finally, making its own wines.

All we have to do is enjoy them...

Top producers

Boekenhoutskloof
Glen Carlou
Delaire
Devon Hill
Neil Ellis
Fairview
Grangehurst
Graham Beck
Hartenberg
Jordan
Kanonkop
Longridge
Meerlust
Plaisir de Merle
Rustenberg
Saxenburg
Thelema
Vriesenhof
Warwick
Welgemeend

For a while in the 1980s, before Australia took the supermarket shelves by storm, the UK fell in love with Bulgarian Cabernet Sauvignon. It was enough to make traditional wine-lovers apoplectic with rage. It was bad enough that the colonials were making wine, but now the Communists were at it as well, and what's more, people were drinking it!

the rest of the world

Look out for

East European reds are sold under varietal name rather than by producer: most are good-value, honest wines.

Bulgaria

It was no surprise that people were drinking it. Cabernet from Bulgaria was packed full of fruit. It smelled of ripe blackberries; it had none of those mouth-drying tannins (though it did have a tingling acidity); it tasted new, fruity, and it was sold at an absurdly low price. The New World of wine, as far as Britain was concerned, started here.

These days things aren't quite so rosy for the Bulgarians. It isn't that the consumer has given up on jammy Cabernets. It isn't that the price has risen – it has stayed remarkably stable. The quality has wobbled, but the main reason has been a loss of volume.

Part of this is due to the allegation that much of what was bottled as Bulgarian Cabernet was actually South African Cabernet shipped in bulk and when South African wine began to be accepted post-apartheid, supplies to Bulgaria dried up. Whether this is true or not we may never know, and it is slightly unfair on an industry that in the 1970s had the foresight to plant huge tracts of land to international varieties like Cabernet, get new wineries funded by the Soviet Union and winemaking expertise courtesy of America. That's some trick.

The problems appeared when Russia stopped importing Bulgarian wine in the early 1990s and many of the vineyards were grubbed up. Then post-Communist messy privatizations confused the issue further, while vineyards were left untended as families fought over the rights to former state-controlled farms. Bulgaria also failed to produce a higher quality range of wines, especially Cabernet, to keep people's interest.

It's clear that the Bulgaria has the potential to make very good (though maybe never great) Cabernet. Now serious investment is needed. The expertise is there. The vines are there but, sadly, it is almost back to square one as far as the public is concerned.

The situation might change as wineries extricate themselves from lingering state control, but you get the feeling that Bulgaria's chance has come and gone. Still, if you want well-priced, sweet, jammy Cabernet, it's still coming up with the goods.

Hungary, Portugal, Austria, & Greece

While Cabernet is grown in Hungary (it is in the blend of that old 1970s staple Bull's Blood), Romania, and Moldova, the variety, for once, hasn't conquered these new territories. The same goes for Portugal, which, with a few exceptions, has persevered with its own varieties. Good, silky Cabernet is made in Ribatejo, Alentejo, and Estremadura. All show concentration, richness of body and lifted perfume.

The reverse seems to have happened in Austria where it has been planted widely but, with a few exceptions in Burgenland, has performed pretty disappointingly, with too many of the wines showing an unripe green character.

Things are slightly better Cabernet-wise in Greece where, although native varieties still dominate plantings, an increasing amount of (good) Cabernet is being produced – another example of a country proving that it is a serious player by planting the aristocrat of red wine. Pioneered by Domaine Carras in the 1970s, it is being perfected at Katsarou and Tselepou, both of which are making excellent, elegant (if stylistically different) wines. The key seems to be the fact that they lie in slightly cooler spots allowing the Cabernet a longer time to ripen. The blazing Greek sun puts paid to much of the rest.

Israel & Lebanon

Israel and Lebanon have extensive plantings of Cabernet Sauvignon. The Israeli wines, predominantly from high vineyards on the Golan Heights and in Galilee, are made

in a rich, soft, quite sweet, Californian style. Dalton
is the name to watch. Prices are high, sadly, but quality
is increasingly good with some individual personality
beginning to appear.

Cabernet takes on a more classical French air in
Lebanon where plantings are concentrated in the Beka'a
Valley. It is blended with Carignan and some Syrah in the
legendary Chateau Musar – a wine that needs a decade
to reveal its elegant gamey core. Increasingly there are
also some richer and more powerful Cabernet-based wines
coming from Château Kefraya and newcomer Massaya.

For me, Lebanon, Greece, and Portugal are the countries
to watch for Cabernet as all have managed to make highly
individual, personal wines that speak of their location
rather than an anonymous international style.

buying, storing, & serving

Get to grips with grape varieties and the fascinating array of flavours and aromas they produce, and you will suddenly know an awful lot more about wine. Here's your guide to Cabernet, plus the lowdown on different blends and tips on buying and serving.

CHATEAU
MOUOY-LALANDE
ST ESTEPHE
ST ESTEPHE CONTRÔLÉE
1997

Whether it's an *extra* special occasion, a decent bottle to take to a dinner party, or just a plain, mid-week pick-me-up, Cabernet can come up with the goods. There is good-value Cabernet to be had at every price level if you know what to look for, and this guide will help you find one to suit your budget.

quality vs price

Bottom-end

There's lots of cheap Cabernet sloshing around. The trouble is that when you pour on the water and increase the amount of grapes on each vine, Cabernet tends to go a bit hard and mean, so be very careful when you buy that bargain-basement bottle. What you have saved in money you might have lost in flavour. Look for Cabernet blends – the Shiraz/Cabernets from South East Australia are decent, simple, fruity wines. Equally, there are still good bargains to be got at this price from Bulgaria.

Mid-market

Not only will you find a wider range here but you'll be getting a much better drop of wine for your money. I'd still remain cautious about buying clarets at this price though. By and large they are likely to be tough and lacking in charm. The good Provence Cabernets are within reach, however, as well as some Italian and Spanish examples. At the upper end you'll find great wines from Lebanon as well as the impressive Cabernets from Greece.

This, however, is where the New World cleans up. New Zealand's increasingly impressive Cabernets are well worth trying, as are those of South Africa, plus you are now hitting a rich vein of richly fruited Australians (Mudgee, McLaren Vale, Barossa, Great Southern). The Californian Cabernets from Lodi/Woodbridge aren't as good value as those from Washington State. The best value of all still comes from that master of consistency, Chile.

Top-end

There's no shortage of wines in this category either, but if you want to start dabbling, go to a reputable wine merchant – and taste as many wines as you can. It's often tempting to invest in a case of young Bordeaux, but please take advice first. Wine merchants will have not just the greatest Bordeaux châteaux but some bargains from lesser-known names.

Do try some of the super-Tuscan wines to see the unique Italian take on the variety. Top Australian Cabernet probably represents the best value for money in this category. The wines are less pricey (and more available) since Shiraz became the hot variety, and there are some world-class wines to be had. There's a host of Californians here, too, but stick to well-established producers rather than taking a punt on a cult wine with a fancy name, a high price tag, and no track record.

The most obvious next step to take on your vinous peregrinations would be to reverse the Cabernet-dominated blends and go for Merlot-dominated ones. In France that means leaving the Médoc and going to St-Emilion, Pomerol, and, should you want great value for money, Côtes de Bourg. Merlot is, generally speaking, softer on the tannin front than Cabernet and its fruitiness is more on the plummy side rather than the blackcurrant. Fleshily voluptuous would be the term to describe it, which is precisely why Merlot is used to tone down Cabernet's often hard edges.

other wines to try

On the other hand, in Merlot/Cabernet blends the latter grape is used to give some grip to those soft fruits. Californian Merlots tend to be slightly firmer than their French equivalents and the best in the USA are still coming from Washington State. Chile makes a great-value soft but chocolatey example.

Cabernet is blended with so many other grapes that it's pretty easy to work out what other varieties to try. After all, if Cabernet likes them, there's a pretty strong likelihood that you will as well. In France take a look at the Cabernet Franc-based reds from the Loire Valley (Bourgueil and Chinon) – all chocolate, red fruits, and a lovely dusty note. It is a variety that performs magnificently in South Africa too, giving a richer style, but still with that gorgeous fragrance. As far as the other Bordeaux varieties go, some inky, spicy, Petit Verdot is beginning to appear from Australia, while the dark, sultry Malbec is the grape of choice in Argentina.

In Spain, Cabernet fans should start with Tempranillo with its lovely mix of chocolate and strawberry, but those who like their wines big and beefy can strike out to Jumilla and discover the dark delights of Monastrell, or inland to Calatayud and Tarragona where the sloe-berry Garnacha rules.

If you like that wilder edge to your wines then keep heading along the Mediterranean coast to the south of France where the same two grapes (now called Monastrell and Grenache) combine with Syrah and Carignan to make wonderfully herbal, peppery, juicy reds. In Italy look for Chianti Classico, all red- and black-cherry; black fruits and smoke from Aglianico in Campania and Basilicata; and the plummy rich Montepulciano d'Abruzzo. While if you venture as far south as Sicily, seek out the island's greatest black grape, Nero d'Avola. More akin to Syrah than Cabernet, but made to the highest quality.

In Greece go for wines made from the Nemean native speciality Agiorghytiko (aka St George). Whatever the country, if you like your reds big and black of fruit, there will be something for you.

The days of having to wait a decade or more before you could drink your Cabernet have long gone. While the great Bordeaux reds will improve in bottle for an amazingly long time, even the Bordelais are making their Cabernet-based wines in a way that makes them more approachable when they are young.

when to serve

So, rather than leaving them for ten years, they can be drunk in five. It's partly down to our lust for instant gratification, but equally it's due to the simple fact that very few of us have cellars in which to stash away those precious bottles.

That said, if you have invested in a top Cabernet from France, California or Oz, it will benefit from a period of ageing. The tannins will soften, the mature aromas – cedar, cigar box, and a gamey note – will emerge. I know, it isn't easy to put your wine away but try and resist temptation. Buy a case, or a half-case, and ration it out over a period of years and see how the wine changes.

While it is always dangerous to generalize, New World Cabernets tend to be ready sooner than top Bordeaux. Part of this is down to the way in which they are made, part is down to the nature (and ripeness) of the fruit. But a word of warning. Just because a wine is big, rich, and heavy doesn't mean it will necessarily age well. Big wines need tannins in the same way that tannic wines need fruit. Once again, balance is crucial.

That's the top-end covered, but mid-market and low-priced Cabernets are there to be drunk as soon as you get the bottle home. These are fruit-filled drinks with low levels of tannin. Get out that corkscrew and open them immediately!

Because Cabernet has become a global grape variety, there are wines not just at every price point, but in a huge range of styles. You'll find Cabernet in wine boxes made for parties, or in posh wooden crates. There is one to suit every occasion.

A great red deserves a great glass. Actually a good red deserves a great glass as well. You want a glass with a long stem and a rounded bowl, large enough for you to be able to swirl your Cabernet around. Then, not only can you see its glorious purple colour but you can fully appreciate its rich, heady aromas as well. That swirling also means that you shouldn't overfill the glass. A third full is perfect. After all, you can always have another glass – and the tablecloth will be spared should that swirling become too animated.

how to serve

What temperature should the wine be served at? Room temperature of course. But what temperature is the room? That sage piece of advice was first coined in the days before central heating had been invented. These days most houses are considerably hotter than they were at the turn of the twentieth century.

I'm not saying that you should treat Cabernet like you should a Beaujolais and pop it briefly in the fridge. Those big, generous fruit flavours – and those big, generous tannins – would not appreciate that sort of treatment. However, neither would they appreciate being kept next to the stove and served not far below boiling point, not unless you and your guests like Cabernet soup.

Basically it is best to serve a Cabernet Sauvignon
at below 22°C (72°F). In fact, I'd suggest that the ideal
temperature is hovering around the 18°–19°C (64-66°F)
mark, which is, you guessed it, likely to be way below the
temperature of your room!

If you have invested in a good Cabernet then it is also
worth investing in a decanter. We all know that a wine –
any wine – needs to breathe, but pulling the cork out
won't do anything other than exposing an area of wine
the size of a small coin to the oxygen. Cabernet, like any
red wine, needs air. So get your decanter and *long* before
you are going to start drinking (two, three hours isn't too
long) pour in the wine. It releases the aromas and makes
for a much more pleasurable drinking experience. It also
looks good! Don't have a decanter? Pour your Cabernet
into a (clean) jug and before your guests arrive decant
it back into the bottle.

It's simple really, whatever you do, enjoy the
experience! There is so much stuffy ritual associated with
wine that we tend to forget that it is there to be enjoyed
in company.

Matching food and wine is a vexed issue and the bottom line is to drink your Cabernet with whatever food you want. Being terrified that you are about to make a terrible *faux pas* will ruin your enjoyment of the wine, and wine and food are there to be enjoyed. That said, here are a few guidelines that might help maximize that pleasure. Hopefully this little book has demonstrated that there is no such thing as one style of Cabernet. There are light Cabernets; soft ones; heavy, thick alcoholic ones; tannic ones. Cabernets that smell of black fruits, others that smell of red fruits. You can get mature, gamey Cabernet and young, black juicy Cabernet.

what to serve with

What is good for one food may be less ideal with another. By and large though, Cabernet doesn't work with spicy foods as this brings the tannins to the fore (but if you have a low-tannin, sweet, and juicy Cabernet, things will be fine). Chinese food is a bit of a disaster area. Cheese can a real problem – stick to stronger cheeses; while fish, especially light fish, will be dominated by the wine.

Where this variety scores is with meat, and red meat especially. Cabernet is a carnivore. Rare meat has the effect of breaking down the tannins. The dark fruit goes magnificently with roasted and grilled meat and with any meat-based sauce. Mature Cabernet with its gamey flavours is a match made in heaven with roast rib of beef, oxtail or, you guessed it, venison or pheasant.

It's equally good with lamb (a mature wine is great here as well, a heavy one less so), but pork can be a bit too light. Mid-priced, New World Cabernet is a great barbeque wine, or goes perfectly with meat stews or mince and potatoes (if you're in Scotland).

Remember the cardinal rule though, the greater the wine, the simpler the food should be.

index